T0130136

# Ria's Heart

Rondamarie Wheatley

**BALBOA.**
PRESS

A DIVISION OF HAY HOUSE

Balboa Press books may be ordered through booksellers or by contacting:

Balboa Press
A Division of Hay House
1663 Liberty Drive
Bloomington, IN 47403
www.balboapress.com
1 (877) 407-4847

Because of the dynamic nature of the Internet, any web addresses or
links contained in this book may have changed since publication and
may no longer be valid. The views expressed in this work are solely those
of the author and do not necessarily reflect the views of the publisher,
and the publisher hereby disclaims any responsibility for them.

The author of this book does not dispense medical advice or prescribe the use
of any technique as a form of treatment for physical, emotional, or medical
problems without the advice of a physician, either directly or indirectly. The
intent of the author is only to offer information of a general nature to help
you in your quest for emotional and spiritual well-being. In the event you use
any of the information in this book for yourself, which is your constitutional
right, the author and the publisher assume no responsibility for your actions.

Any people depicted in stock imagery provided by Thinkstock are
models, and such images are being used for illustrative purposes only.
Certain stock imagery © Thinkstock.

Print information available on the last page.

ISBN: 978-1-5043-8687-6 (sc)
ISBN: 978-1-5043-8688-3 (e)

Library of Congress Control Number: 2017913343

Balboa Press rev. date: 11/02/2017

This book is dedicated in memory of my father,
William J. Wheatley, and to my son, Kendall L. Harris.

# Acknowledgements

I wrote so many poems in 1986. I'm thankful for so many who have crossed my path with learning lessons. Thanks be to God for the creation of my presence on this earth. Thanks to nuns and priests of St. Anselms Parish who helped mold my character from the mid 1950s to the 1960s. My family, who always believed in me, who have gone to be with the Lord. My dear sister and friend, Lela Marie Long, who always gave me encouragement and my guardian angels and the universe. A special thanks to Myra West-Allen for her support and computer editing skills.

Life has truly been what my parents and elders told me it would be.

When you're young you feel like your life is forever and the old folks don't know anything.

Because they are old and they can't do anything. Not realizing they had to be young first.

Now I am the elder with the youth giving me the same look I used to give. So many of my family, friends, and loved ones are now gone to be with the Lord.

Those who would take the time to listen and give their opinion even when they were in the midst of other things, they would listen to the poems I wrote.

I believe in the law of attraction and even though my poems of life were mine, I knew one day I would publish them, as I would be living my golden years in Georgia.

Well the day has come. Thanks be to God my dream has come true.

I've had many, during the years, who have traveled on the road of my words.

I hope you are touched in some way by my writing. Perhaps there may be words that have been walkways of your life. I thank God for my journey and I'm still moving on.

For all who may read this book, may God keep and bless you always.

As my grandmother would say when she talked about being grown, "Honey, it ain't what you think it is.

Ria

# The Meeting of Two Souls

A single rose at introduction,
A tender kiss behind the scene,
Dinner and the best of champagne,
A tender touch that drew our souls together, like water to land.
The electricity gave a full current when you held my hand.
Our bodies unaware of our souls
Uniting as one before our secret affair.
So mystical it had seemed to be;
As you looked in my eyes and saw through me
The soul you've been searching for across the sea.
The sparkling lit fireplace gave warmth and a glow.
We held each other; there was no place we wanted to go.
The meeting of souls can be deep
As we held each other and fell asleep.

# Men, or Whatever You Call Them

Men, boys, males—
Whatever you call them.
Big, small, medium;
What the hell: they're all the same.
When you tried one,
You've tried them all.
Hurting a woman's feelings is what they call having a ball
They use your mind and your body if they can.
And when you realize it, they don't call, and they stand you up
    once again..
You stop and regroup and say never, no more.
You get older, and this game starts to become a bore!

# The Spirit of a California Man

Free spirit, free spirit is what you are,
Never staying too long or going too far.
Like the winds that blow, you fly by your life,
Never stopping to see stress or strife.
So light and soft, at times you seem,
But moving with the ray of light or a beam.
Stop sometimes, and let me see
The free spirited man that you appear to be.

# Sitting

As I sit here day after day,
I look for happiness and peace in just some small way.
The world seems to be rushing every day.
Stop moving so fast; slow down, now and then, in some kind of way.
We all will end up at the same old place,
Some six feet of dirt with a stone for a face.
So what's the hurry?
The hustle and bustle, to and fro.
Slow down, take your time, you will end up below.

# The Good Ole Days

When I was just a sweet young girl, about sixteen and a half,
I knew those were the real good old days; wasn't nothin' better than.
I said one day a man would come and sweep me off my feet,
And surely one day he would come along.
But he wasn't mine to keep.
Oh … the good old days are memories.
Oh, the good old days are sweet.
Just always keep in the back of your mind that
A good man's hard to keep.
As time moved on and I had fun, or so I heard it said,
My grandma said, slow down, young girl,
Or you will end up dead.
She said one day the right man will come, and it'll take you by surprise,
But if you don't slow down, young girl,
He'll be gone right before your eyes.
But the good ole days are memories,
And the good ole days are sweet.
But never forget I told you that a good man is hard to keep.

# The J. C. Spirit

It took me over like a natural high.
I wondered what was happening to me and why.
I remembered I heard Grandma say,
"The Lord will bless and keep your soul one day."
Grandma said, "Just trust in him,
And he will shine a light on you
When yours grows dim."
She said, "God can lift you up even when there's no food
And an empty cup."
And praise God, Grandma's words are true.
I've been down and out, and the Lord has pulled me through.
If you've never heard of these words from this grandma of mine,
Read again these lines of mine.
Praise God, the Lord divine.
Now to all, I give my grandma's words to you.
Trust in God; I'm an example of what God can do.
Now I'm thirty-one and excited about this feeling.
Not by alcohol, a disco light, or a limelight life.
I'm batting a thousand through Jesus Christ.
Not wealthy, not a star in movies or on TV,
But God has held, loved, and taken care of me.

## Someone for Me

I asked God to send me someone kind and true,
And he sent me you.
Someone to have and someone to hold,
Someone who cared to shelter me from the cold.
And he sent you.
I asked God to send me someone to make me laugh and smile
At the sunshine all day long.
And bless and behold, you came along.
But there's such a gap between you and me.
Sometimes I wonder if once again
I'll be lonely …
I want to enjoy the rest of my life with you,
But you, my loved one, must want it too.
Our time on this earth is short, I must say.
That's why it's important for us to enjoy each day.

# Working for the City

You must live in the city is what your rules say.
I'm afraid to go in and out of my apartment each and every day.
I'm a single parent, trying to make it on my own.
It's bad enough the president has taken away the dream of owning
    a home.
I would like to live in a clean and decent environment
Just like you.
Except by myself, not a guard or two.
Questions they ask: are you married? is one; if not, no need to fill
    out the application.
Look at the apartments and condos they give.
Fabulous with luxury in the suburbs to live.
But I need my job because jobs are hard to come by and few,
And I want my child to see more than just an alley view.
When you raise taxes and shuffle the budget awhile,
Think of us single women and our children.
Now, as you end your day, as we do too.
Think if the shoes I walk in belonged to you.
Standing at the meat counters is like, looking at jewelry diamond
    counter.
Picking up and then putting back because it's too high.
It's trying to survive and not stand there and cry.
Turning on the TV, looking at others' points of view.

You start turning the channel to 7, 5, and 2.

Then you cut it off because now you're really blue.

You get up in the morning, wanting to buy a paper

To see what it was last night that they said.

But you don't want to read that you lost your job while you were
in bed.

Now as you end your day, as we all do,

Stop and think if the shoes I walked in belonged to you.

# Mayor Washington

A smile that takes you back home,
A man who is noble, like an emperor of Rome,
A man who seems gentle and makes you want to touch.
But this man has so much success, just so much!
There are many secret powers he has within.
But only those who have depth of feeling know about them.
Some people played his intelligence cheaply, and that was their mistake.
Mayor Washington showed them all he was one they could not break.
Let what he has gone through show us all;
Let all men stand up and be proud.
Give respect to the big and the small.
Let's respect one another; that's the least we can do.
Look back and remember the turmoil Mayor Washington went
    through.

## My Buddy

We came such a long way.
Like sisters we always were.
The love, the kindness, the tender loving care
You wrapped around me like fur.
I always felt warm and safe with you close to me.
But now you show me little affection.
Like a bare branch on a tree, its cold winds blowing through me.
In a very special way, I stand in the shadows, waiting to hear you
    say the words that were said when we were young:
We will always be together, forever and a day.

# Nigerian Love

A plant sitting in a cold clay pot, still trying to hold on, trying to
get a glimpse of sunlight from an airy window, just a small
thing to try and survive.

Life across the continent put a closure to your only love being
young to old and laid it to rest.
Aaaah, and even in another world sits another plant of life, trying
not to wither into death.
The universe made it possible to bring you from one continent to
another, traveling such a long way, sending you to me through
a system neither of us were comfortable with.

So hesitant and afraid,
We both, of a scam, afraid of hurt, afraid to love again, only to be
hurt by our emotions.
As we became closer and closer each day, we finally reached our
day of passion, our day of passion.
As the liquid left your hose of life and ran into the valley of my
well—
Being that it had become dry and had a feeling of uselessness—
You lovingly parted the dry earth and emptied the wetness that
you still had.
And the plant? Yes, the plant that had begun withering started
coming back to life, once again producing the womanly scent
of a flower; yes, the flower that you —the man who was once
dying so long, long ago—once again began to live.

# A Friend like You

A friend like you, something to have.
When things are low, you make me laugh.
When I'm depressed and pushed to weep,
I think of you, a friend to keep.
First through grammar school and then through high.
Although we're grown we see each other by and by.
And when we get old and get Medicare, we can think of the good
times we did share.

# Little Walter

I liked Walter; he was really a nice kid.
But there were things I didn't like that Little Walter did.
I didn't know a lot about him; a friend of my son's, I do know
To see him die in the street hurt me so!
He was some mother's child, just like mine is to me.
No longer does he have to play the game of life to be.
There is no life for him to look forward to; he's gone now and
    forever to leave his friend blue.
Maybe, Walt, just maybe this was supposed to be.
Not once did I get to say thanks for always looking out for me.
Standing on the corner that I fussed to you and mine so.
The same place you died, where I watched your blood flow.
Always a smile, and, "Hello, Ms. Harris," you would say.
I pray, little Walt, that your soul is at rest still today.

# If You Knew

No one knows the hurt inside
Skin and flesh can make our feelings hide
Laughing, joking, and talking.
But deep inside, my feelings are hidden by the outer skin and flesh
A smile I'll show you, just to make you think I am at my best.
But no one knows the hurt inside, skin and flesh can make our
    feelings hide.
Fooling them and fooling you.
Laughing, talking, and joking and trying to prove something too!
Proving that what you don't know won't hurt you.
And if it did, someone would know about the hurt inside,
And how you can make your feelings hide.

# Meeting

You're not getting any younger an old man said
The night he winked at me and tried to take me to bed
He talked of his experiences and money made on his job,
I started talking about my problems, he told me about the day he
    got robbed.
Here, have another drink or maybe two.
And before we get to know each other better, I'll pick up some
    barbecue.
You're someone I can talk to, not at all like my wife.
I asked how long have been with her?
He replied, Oh, most of my life.
She doesn't look sexy not even in bed.
Every night there's that scarf on her head!
No, she's nothing like you I must say
You're sexy and easy to talk to; you have a special way.
"Well, I have children, and bills that must be paid
I'm not making enough at work and it's impossible to save.
I'm glad I'm easy to talk to, and I'm crazy about you too
But other than compare me to your wife, what else can you do?

# Grandma

Grandma, I hope you can see what I'm trying to be.

Grandma, I hope you can see just what you instilled in me.

It would be so nice, if only I knew you could see, I'm very honored
to be an extension from your tree.

Please Lord let her see, it was like you said, toil and strife.

But you were right this is a part of life.

When I look up and see a star, I hope it's a sign of your happiness
shining.

The shining twinkle afar.

# Great Boy

Poor little boy, you seem so sad and blue,
At times I sit and wonder did I do wrong by having you.
I wanted the best for you to have, but the task has been hard trying
on my behalf.
You have a father but only in name.
Poor little great boy don't ever feel ashamed.
You can be better or best at what you do.
Just keep in mind, God and Mama both love you.

# The Dream

The dream I have wanted for life
Was to meet someone like you, and be your wife.
The fire was there when I first saw your face.
This is where my love is to take place.
Strong as the winds, calm as the seas,
Lord, let me be his wife please …
So long I've waited for this dream to come true
A real and sincere love I found in you.
As I sit and day dream all day long,
I hope and pray that this love is not wrong.
Thoughts of us together; our kisses of passion so sweet.
It's what I've always dreamed of, from the man I did meet.

# MROW

Don't leave me out here, "I'm afraid
Who wouldn't be round these graves?
The dark, the cold, and the old tombstones
The wind, the moon and some old bones.
The crackin' gates swinging back and forth
And people now and then on Memorial Day and July Fourth.

Don't walk on me, it's bad enough
Hey don't litter, I've had it rough.
You bring flowers and flags.
But that's not for me!
I need more than that you see!
I'm a worm?

# LEONA

L ... is for lovely and loving as you are
E ... is for enthusiastic and enriched with elements from afar
O ... is for only one of a kind
N ... is for natural like grapes from the vine
A ... is for always you'll stay in my heart
LEONA ... my mother and life's spark

# *Untitled*

I've done all I can do,

To keep the peace of a family of a few.

As each elder makes their exit to the great beyond; it makes more
   distance and less compassion with the family bond.

Why are they gone?

The family knew, those who are left have no bond.

No compassion, no love, no helping hand.

Only what can you give me? Here I stand

Asking for what you got, so what if you worked for it!

This is the world of haves and the haves not.

# Shoes

I wore the shoes of being a lover

Then I put on the pair of being a mother

Then I had to wear a pair of a man and a father

And, oh, those that felt tight, the tight fit I wore on the job to provide for us as a family.

After you began having your own thoughts and opinions, I had to get out the pair of the disciplinarian.

Sometimes I could slip on a pair for a few minutes just to be me, but in this world you would need to know a lot as you went forward in life to become a man.

A woman to wear a pair of shoes for a man, in hopes to show her son it's hard because men don't fit well on females' feet.

But I wore them anyway and I did the best that I could.

I also had a pair I wore because I was a daughter, a pair being a sister, and many for being a good friend.

In life you walk in certain shoes for various occasions.

How did you fill all those shoes girl?

And now that you are old, just how do your feet feel?

How do my feet feel, you ask?

Well, no one ever really looked closely at my shoes and my feet have walked many a mile. Now some days I don't put on stocking or socks.

I soak my feet, put cream on them and show them plenty of love.

They've done a lot of walking, and now deserve to rest with me for a while.

# A Mother's Heart

I'm sorry you never felt that I was a good mother.
I tried and did the best that I could.
You were my first and only.
No book of directions came with you
Just a baby when the doctor said "Push!"
Then there was you.
Being a single mother is a hard road to travel, especially when a
    male child is conceived.
As you grew, I played the role of so many it's hard to believe.
Our years were only twenty apart; I was mentally a child myself,
    with a baby and a broken heart.
As years went by reaching puberty, teens, and a man.
I tried so hard to keep you from those who didn't have your best
    interest at hand.
The anger you held on to and kept in your heart.
I continue to pray for you and me because God knows the truth
    about a mother's heart.

# Pimping Hard

Diamond in the back, he rode with a sunroof top
He always drove the scene with a gangster lean and died.
Coke sniffin', cocaine shootin', reefer smokin', pill droppin', and died.
Small time pimpin', mean dealin', big time boostin', Cadillac
    drivin', diamond rings and big money carryin'.
And he died.

# Martin Luther King

Hey Martin! Hey Martin!
Hey Martin Luther King!
I sit here years later, now telling my son about your dream.
Hey Martin, no Martin.
I haven't forgotten you yet.
The protests and marches are nothing to regret.
A great leader, one who won respect and faith from his people.
Oh no Martin, we could never forget.
I saw you leave here, you just walked on away with God, but what
    you left with me was strength and more belief in Him.
You said you've been to mountaintop and I know I'm on way there.
I hope we, as a people, accomplish what you wanted us to!
They're talking about a holiday
Which is or isn't right
But just like anything for Blacks, our people must continue to fight.
Fight for what is due us
And what was always true
Fighting for civil rights, and keeping dignity and respect too.
Yeah, they're talking about a holiday, your birthday is on its way
And no matter what they do
Your birthday, our holiday, shall always be recognized and
    celebrated from me to you.

# My So Called Friend

My so called friend, you pretended to be
Not knowing I knew you never cared for me.
The task you performed with the help of a man.
I succeeded alone, with a single hand.
It makes me laugh; it makes me cry
The game you played as a friend makes me wonder why when I
    complete a task
Which I've always been known to do
I see the look of envy from your face, from you.

Let me offer some advice which is free from me to you.
Try getting yourself a life; things would be much better for you.
Why stand there and wonder
What surprises I will come up with next
I'll be living my own life and doing my best.

# See Him Again

I thought I had found love; once again it wasn't true
I hadn't seen you in eleven years and you popped up out of the blue.
You said it must be fate that brought us back together this way.
But is it you or is it fate that I started hating today?
You had me fooled and deeply in love, I must say
Was it you or was it love I wanted to stay?
I felt like a lonely soldier who was wounded when you said goodbye.
The walls, cold and still, watched me all night
While walking the floors trying to wipe the hurt away that made
    me cry.
It makes me wonder, what was all this for?
I was hurt twice in life by you, but never no more.
I still believe there's someone for me, but I'll always wonder what
    is up his sleeve.
There's nothing about me that looks for hurt or pain,
After this, may I never see you again.
You said you missed me.
What a shock after so many years you looked for me too.
I should have known this was too good to be true.
Now I sit here alone three weeks later.
I understand why I'm blue; I just gave you too much credit, credit not
    due to you. There may be a time when we'll see each other again.
And when the tables turn you may need my love my friend.
The love I have left may be gone by then.

# Mama

I wish I could talk to you
Like grandma said I should
I wish you could have been understanding
Like grandma could
I tried to talk to you, in every kind of way
But you really never understood or talked like they did in grandma's day.
I never felt comforted or at peace with you
And now I'm grown and there's nothing we can do.
I regret a lot of days that have passed us both by.
I used to sit on grandma's bed and ask her why.
Why can't I feel what people said I should feel for you?
And you said you had to leave for a while; this was something you had to do.
I guess a while became longer than we both thought
And when you returned to get me it was grandma's love, not yours, that I sought.
Now I don't want to hurt you or make you blue
This is how things turn out when there is something else you want to do.

# Aunt Evelyn

Dear Aunt Evelyn, quiet and serene.
More like a person in a dream
Always had something nice to say
Even if, maybe, auntie had a bad day.
Forever baking cakes and pies, always with a smile
I know she loved me, well that's true
But there is not too much more I remember of you.
You had a daughter named Marvel, but she doesn't remind me of
    you at all.
Sorry to say, you departed this earth and went on your way
I know dear Aunt Evelyn I'll see you again someday.

# Wind Blowing

Winds blowing soft and cool
Making me take in deeper breaths of air that I long for.
The coolness and wetness of the Lord's tears
The cold water making my body feel like a sponge from the
    ocean's floor.
So saturated, I'm overflowing but how I want more.
The smell of dirt from which I came
Let it trickle through my fingers, one day I'll return to it again.
Reaching and stretching my hands out to you
I didn't want to leave this earth, Lord what shall I do?
They say when you're born only destined to die'I sit upon the
    banks and ask the Lord why?
We always become so close and let love suck us in
Like the cat with the mouse
When the cat is charming him
The curtain is up and the finale to begin
Our friends become saddened because it is the end.

# *Minnie*

Dear Minnie

One of the first ladies in my life. Taking me to the park, skating, and watching the boys play basketball in the courtyard. Her lipstick red as could be and fingernail polish, oh, too red for me.

Dearest Minnie, she made 97 today, looked into my eyes and said, "The Lord is on His way."

The memories of her and her time she gave to me, is why I could never forget Minnie.

Minnie White

# Got to Move Up

I've got to move up
Can't keep standing here with an empty cup
What is it; what is it I need?
I need a better life
A life with a better breed.
But I'm just one Black woman around here.
One who lives in danger and with fear.
One who works and sleepless nights
Scared that one day the gangs may fight.
Why can't we live with love and peace
Instead of hate and violence in the street.
We all have to walk those who are young and old
Let's all have warmth in our hearts instead of being cold.
I've got to move up
Can't keep standing here
I've had it and I'm tired of living in fear.

# Grandma & Grandpa

"I'm going up yonder," is what my folks must have been singing
When the time came to see my Lord.

The air crisp and brisk,
Sunlight beaming from above each time
One of them went to see my Lord.

I was strong and held my head up high
Each time one had went beyond the skies.
When they went to see my Lord.

Now my days are long and lonely
My memories are constantly entwined in my mind
And when the air is crisp and brisk and the sunlight is sunny and bright
I smile and look up toward the skies
Way up, way up yonder.

# Look

Do you know what you see?
When you look into the eyes of me?
Love, hurt, hate, and pain.
This is what man has given to me; again and again
Like rain.

# Cous, oh, cous

We who were brought up right
Now are one of many who may become ladies of the night The
     folks are all gone
The end to them with no beginning
The children who have gotten hungry
Are too big now, to just sit and be grinning
The jobs are scarce, far and end between
The bills are overdue
And having a home of our own, was only just a dream
The mental bricks which were given to us
To build our sturdy wall
Has been torn down
Like nothing had been built at all
We played as kids
Planning and building our future
We could be whatever we wanted to be
Do whatever we wanted to do with an education
But oh, Cous
I believe we were brought up right
Principles and morals were the in things, then in our sight
And I will always believe in them until I pass away one night.

# The Death of You

I can't believe what I've heard,
The Death of you
No my love this can't be true.
The Death of you
The plans, the dream we both had.
Can't now just be a thing that's passed.
But since you're gone, I miss you so.
I lay at night and toss and turn.
And keep your memory, that I still yearn.
I feel you with me day and night.
And hoping soon that we'll unite.
"They say go on, that I'll survive."
But It's so hard now that you're not alive.
It won't be long, I can't wait!
This will be something to celebrate!
It's been three weeks since you died.
And every day of the week I have cried.
The tears are gone, no more shall I cry.
I think it's time I said
                    GOOD-BYE.

# Peace

Peace, be still
I wonder if it ever will
Life is like being twisted on a torture wheel
Peace, sweet peace be still.
Peace, peace be still
The wondering is gone
And I've found the will.
The will to live
And the will to survive
Accepting Jesus as my Savior
Now born again and alive
Peace, be still
Peace, be still
Oh, such a sweet peace
Peace, peace, peace
Be still.

# Thank You

Thank you Lord, my day was tough
Thank you Lord, my road was rough
Thank you Lord, for smoothing my day
Thank you Lord, for guiding my way
Thank you Lord, for the places I've been
Thank you Lord, for not letting my enemies in
Thank you Lord, for the laughter and the tears
Thank you Lord, for all my years.

# Lonely and Blue

Lord I'm tired, lonely, and blue
I sit here day by day, scared to death not knowing what to do.
They say this is America, land of the free!
But when they said it, did they forget about me?
To live in a decent neighborhood you to be making this or that.
You go to the supermarket, just looking at meat makes you fat.
Lord, I'm tired, lonely, and blur.
Thank you for staying with me, to pull me through.
I've been climbing your mountain, year by year.
One day I will be home with you, the one who's been so dear.
I've cried tears and you wiped them and made me smile
I've sweated and toiled and you wiped my brow.
Lord I've struggled, it's alright you see.
I will never fall except to you on my knees.

# Sister Mariam

Goodbye!

I'll see you in heaven, as she walked away,

A smile I'll never forget.

Dressed like a penguin, a portly figure at that.

I was as special to her as she was to me.

When I became grown I tried to reach her, but was told she had
    died, was in heaven — her new home.

Kind and gentle, soft spoken as such, a teacher of mine I thought
    of so much.

Sister Mariam

Printed in the United States
By Bookmasters